THIS BOOK BELONGS TO

_____

STONE

For Oscar and Max
BL

"Curiosity is the beginning of
all wisdom." For Albie the wise.
With love,
GBS

Text copyright © 2023 by Ben Lerwill
Illustrations copyright © 2023 by Grahame Baker-Smith

First US edition 2023
First published by Walker Books Ltd. (UK) 2023

Library of Congress Catalog Card Number pending
ISBN 978-1-5362-3134-2

CCP 28 27 26 25 24 23
10 9 8 7 6 5 4 3 2 1

Printed in Shenzhen, Guangdong, China

This book was typeset in Din.
The illustrations were done in mixed media.

Candlewick Press
99 Dover Street
Somerville, Massachusetts 02144

www.candlewick.com

AGE BEASTS

Ben Lerwill

illustrated by

Grahame Baker-Smith

CANDLEWICK PRESS

CONTENTS

WELCOME TO THE STONE AGE

It's almost three million years ago. Prehistoric forests cloak the land, giant beasts roam the hills, and living among them are humans. Still learning about the world around them, our ancestors have just started making and using stone tools. This is the dawn of the Stone Age.

Our planet has been spinning through space for about 4.5 billion years. For a long, long time, there wasn't much to see. The air became breathable 2.5 billion years ago, and the earliest dinosaurs evolved much later, around 250 million years ago.

Long after dinosaurs went extinct, our early human ancestors appeared in Africa five to seven million years ago. But it wasn't until nearly three million years ago that humans started shaping stones into tools such as axes, knives, hammers, scrapers, and arrowheads.

WHAT DID THE WORLD LOOK LIKE DURING THE STONE AGE?

The Stone Age ended only about 4,000 years ago, so it saw the planet go through many changes. In the distant past, the world map that we know today would have looked very different. At times, there were higher sea levels, hotter temperatures, and less land. The Stone Age also had long periods of extreme cold—known as ice ages—with warm periods in between. It meant the lands were sometimes green and wild and sometimes icy and frozen. And just like today, different parts of the world had different climates.

STONE AGE HUMANS

Stone Age humans were hunter-gatherers, surviving by hunting, fishing, and gathering plants and fruit. Over millions of years, they spread around the world, learning new things and making new discoveries. They didn't have the kinds of buildings, clothes, and machines that we have today, but they were highly intelligent. They learned how to communicate with one another and live together. In many places they also began farming the land to grow food.

Using different tools—made from stone, wood, plants, and animal parts—Stone Age humans were able to make their lives easier. Animal bones could be carved into knives, spoons, needles, necklaces, and fishhooks.

They made fire by striking flint stones together or by using a hand-turned wooden drill. Fire was used to keep warm, to cook food, and to scare away animals.

They carved wood to make bowls, spears, and other useful things. For example, a bull-roarer was a small piece of wood attached to a rope. When it was whirled around in fast circles, it made a very loud noise. Experts think bull-roarers were used to scare away large creatures!

They used animal skins to make clothing and shelter.

MEET THE ANIMALS

For Stone Age humans, survival was about much more than using tools. They shared the lands, rivers, and seas with beasts of all shapes and sizes. Early humans needed to be excellent hunters and trappers. Animals provided meat, skins, and bones—all of which were vital resources.

HOW DID HUMANS CATCH STONE AGE ANIMALS?

Hunters could use spears, clubs, or bows and arrows to kill a wild animal. Spears and arrows were made by attaching sharpened stones or bones to wooden sticks. Bows were made by tying rope or animal sinew to bendy sticks, or even to long bones.

Stone Age humans also caught fish. They used traps and nets or waded into the water with a harpoon, a kind of spear with a barbed, pointed tip.

Groups of armed hunters could hide and ambush larger creatures. Some experts think that early humans used dogs to help them catch their prey—and we know that some big beasts were killed by being chased into pits, ponds, or traps, or even off cliffs.

Hunting was risky, but it was worth it. One large kill might feed a family for months, and any spare meat could be dried and saved for later.

WHAT DID HUMANS THINK OF THESE ANIMALS?

Every part of the world had different birds, mammals, and reptiles. We know from ancient cave paintings that humans were aware of the creatures that lived around them. Some large animals would have been seen as very dangerous and others as rivals because they ate the same food that humans did. But early humans would also have respected and maybe even worshipped some of these huge beasts. No one knows for sure why some Stone Age animals were so large, but one theory is that when dinosaurs died out, there were more plants for land mammals to feed on. Because there was more food, different species of plant-eaters adapted to become bigger and stronger over thousands of years. And the predators that hunted them adapted and became bigger, too!

There's so much that we'll never know about the Stone Age and the humans and wildlife that lived alongside one another. What we do know is that all over the world, there were giant animals that once called our planet home. So let's meet the extinct prehistoric creatures who roamed the earth with our ancestors.

WOOLLY MAMMOTH

FOUR TREE-TRUNK LEGS. TWO TWIRLY TUSKS. ONE HAIRY HEAD.

Meet the woolly mammoth, one of the biggest and heaviest of all the Stone Age beasts. Can you imagine the noise and smell of seeing one up close? Today we use the word *mammoth* to mean "very big," which is no surprise—those huge feet would have made the earth shake!

SCIENTIFIC NAME
Mammuthus primigenius

WEIGHT
Up to 16,000 pounds (7,300 kg)

WHEN DID IT BECOME EXTINCT?
Around 4,000 years ago

WHERE DID IT LIVE?
Northern Europe, northern Asia, and North America

Mammoths might have been ENORMOUS, but they wouldn't have tried to eat you. These hefty herbivores survived on grass, leaves, shrubs . . . and lots of flowers! Being so large, they needed to eat massive amounts every day.

Walking over snow and ice can be difficult, but mammoths had a way of making it easier. The bottoms of their feet had big cracks in them—just like the soles of your sneakers have grips— and this stopped them from slipping.

A woolly mammoth was about the same
size as a modern African elephant, but its extra-long
tusks and fleecy coat made it a very different animal.
It lived in the cold of the Ice Age, so it had thick hair to
keep it warm and relatively small ears that wouldn't
get frozen in the chill. Scientists think it used its curved
tusks to sweep snow and ice away to find food . . .
and to battle other mammoths!

Stone Age humans had to work together to hunt
mammoths. Sometimes they chased them off
cliffs! Sometimes they used spears, but this was
dangerous, as the animal could trample them if
frightened. A mammoth provided a huge amount
of meat, and its bones, tusks, and coat could all be
used to make tools and clothes.

ELEPHANT BIRD

PICTURE A BIRD AS TALL AS TWO PEOPLE AND AS HEAVY AS A GRAND PIANO, with eggs larger than any dinosaur's. For thousands of years, the elephant bird lumbered through the steamy rain forests of Madagascar like a supersize ostrich. It was flightless and had a conical beak as big as a witch's hat. It weighed more than any other bird in history.

Scientists think it moved slowly, chomping plants. A bit too slowly, maybe. Humans arrived on the island as long as 10,000 years ago, and we know that when elephant birds wandered too far from their nests, hunters would have seen their giant eggs as easy food.

Unlike some large animals on Madagascar, the elephant bird itself was rarely hunted by humans. Our ancestors seemed to have respected the bird—even though they were happy to take its eggs!

Elephant bird eggs were about a foot long (more than 30 centimeters) and heavier than a hundred chicken eggs put together! One egg would have fed many humans. Amazingly, some of these gigantic eggs still exist today. In 2013, an unhatched elephant bird egg sold for more than $100,000!

There are different theories about why the elephant bird became extinct. Egg-stealing is just one of them. The first people on Madagascar also brought chickens with them, which some experts think would have introduced dangerous bird diseases. And when the island's thick jungle started to be cleared by humans, elephant birds lost their natural habitat and became even rarer, until finally there were none left at all.

SCIENTIFIC NAME
Aepyornis maximus

WEIGHT
Around 1,000 pounds (450 kg)

WHEN DID IT BECOME EXTINCT?
About 1,000 years ago

WHERE DID IT LIVE?
Madagascar

GIANT SHORT-FACED BEAR

WARNING: DO NOT APPROACH THIS BEAR.

With its loping legs, muscly forearms, and savage snout, the giant short-faced bear was fast, furry, and frighteningly fierce. It roamed North America during the last ice age, eating whatever meaty meal it could lay its paws on. It was strong enough to crush bones with its jaws and speedy enough to chase down deer and wild horses. It was also bigger than any bear living today, and on its hind legs it was almost twice as tall as an adult man. Early humans who migrated from Russia to North America probably had quite a fright when they saw the giant short-faced bear—and its teeth—for the first time!

SCIENTIFIC NAME
Arctodus simus

WEIGHT
Around 1,500 pounds (700 kg)

WHEN DID IT BECOME EXTINCT?
Around 11,000 years ago

WHERE DID IT LIVE?
North America

Some scientists say that the giant short-faced bear was a bit lazy, preferring to scavenge the meals of other animals rather than hunt. It would have used its sharp sense of smell to track down kills made by smaller predators, then chased them off and filled its belly.

This bear was a hypercarnivore, which means it needed to eat a lot of meat—around 35 pounds (16 kilograms) a day (the equivalent of around 190 sausages!).

Some of the first humans to reach North America were the Clovis people, who are well known for their flint spearheads. It's possible that these humans, together with the arrival of brown bears from Europe and Asia, caused the giant short-faced bear to become extinct because they were all competing for the same prey.

WONAMBI

LET'S SLITHER 65 MILLION YEARS BACK IN TIME,

to when dinosaurs roamed the planet. Giant snakes lived in many different parts of the world, including Africa, Europe, and South America. Some were as long as school buses! By the Stone Age, they weren't quite so huge, but some terrifying species existed, including the deadly Australian serpent known as Wonambi. And what a snake it was. From scaly tail to slippery tongue it measured about 20 feet (6 meters), with fangs as sharp as pins. It hunted prehistoric animals by wrapping tightly around them and squeezing the breath from their bodies. Australia's earliest humans would have seen these huge snakes as a threat, so maybe it's no surprise that experts think Wonambi became extinct soon after people arrived.

SCIENTIFIC NAME
Wonambi naracoortensis

WEIGHT
About 110 pounds (50 kg)

WHEN DID IT BECOME EXTINCT?
Around 50,000 years ago

WHERE DID IT LIVE?
Australia

Indigenous Australians have lived on the island for tens of thousands of years. They have many legends about godlike creatures that helped to shape the land—and one of them is about a rainbow serpent called Wonambi.

Wonambi's teeth weren't just sharp. They were also curved, like the thorns on a rose. For any animal being eaten by the snake, these curved fangs made escape nearly impossible.

Wonambi wasn't a venomous snake, so it had to choose its prey carefully. It probably hid near trees, rocks, or bushes, then sprung out to coil around its victims. Very large animals would have been too hard to catch, but smaller kangaroos and wallabies would have been just right for a filling meal.

GIGANTOPITHECUS

A GRUNT IN THE DARKNESS. A RUSTLE IN THE TREES. Then out of the woods steps an enormous creature with an enormous name: *Gigantopithecus*. This towering ape was a true giant of the Stone Age, a hairy hulk that moved through the forests of Asia on all fours. Standing upright, it was almost twice as tall as a human.

By studying fossils of its teeth and jaws, scientists have worked out that *Gigantopithecus* was a plant-eater. Its powerful arms could grab huge handfuls of leaves and fruit, just like today's gorillas, and its teeth were good for chewing and grinding. We don't know if *Gigantopithecus* was fierce or friendly, but if it became angry, it would definitely have been best to back away!

What do you think early humans would have thought when they first spotted a *Gigantopithecus* in the trees? These people were actually related to the giant creatures—just like we are to today's chimps and gorillas—but they outlived them because, unlike *Gigantopithecus*, humans could adapt to different diets and environments.

Gigantopithecus lived close to areas of open grassland, but it chose to stay in the shelter of the woods, where it was easier to find a meal. The forest also provided more protection from the tropical weather. Over many years, the temperatures became cooler and the forests started to disappear, which is probably why the creature became extinct.

Gigantopithecus would have had a gigantic appetite. Some scientists think that it mainly ate bamboo, as today's pandas do, but others believe it would have eaten many kinds of forest foods, from leaves and roots to berries and hanging fruits.

SCIENTIFIC NAME
Gigantopithecus blacki

WEIGHT
Up to about 600 pounds (270 kg)

WHEN DID IT BECOME EXTINCT?
Around 100,000 years ago

WHERE DID IT LIVE?
China and Southeast Asia

SABER-TOOTHED CAT

THIS IS ONE CAT YOU DEFINITELY WOULDN'T WANT ON YOUR LAP.

With its terrifying teeth and powerful paws, the saber-toothed cat—or *Smilodon*—was a predator to fear. It prowled North and South America until around 10,000 years ago, using its formidable strength to bring down creatures far bigger than itself. Though its short legs made it slow in the chase, it was stealthy enough to be an expert at ambushing prey—and no human or animal would have relished being surprised by *Smilodon*.

Its two longest teeth would have been used for stabbing and slashing prey, and the creature also had incredibly strong neck muscles. So be careful. This kitty might bite!

For *Smilodon*, the menu of the day would be any animal unlucky enough to be in the wrong place at the wrong time. As well as feasting on deer, this hypercarnivore most likely also hunted sloths, bison, and maybe even young mammoths. *Smilodon*'s front teeth could grow to 11 inches (28 centimeters) long—that's longer than a pencil!

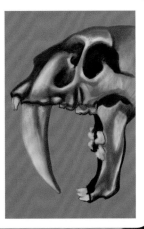

Smilodon often gets described as a saber-toothed tiger, or even a saber-toothed lion, but it wasn't closely related to today's big cats. It was actually part of a unique animal group, and some varieties were smaller than modern lions, even though they could weigh more than twice as much!

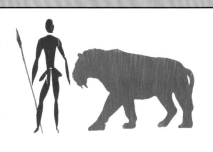

SCIENTIFIC NAME
Smilodon

WEIGHT
Up to 1,000 pounds (450 kg)

WHEN DID IT BECOME EXTINCT?
Around 10,000 years ago

WHERE DID IT LIVE?
North and South America

We don't know why *Smilodon* became extinct. At the end of the last ice age, temperatures started rising. Maybe the climate changed too quickly for them to adapt. And early humans, who may have competed for some of the same prey, could also have contributed to the disappearance of these huge predators.

GIANT SHORT-FACED KANGAROO

THINK OF A KANGAROO. WHAT DO YOU SEE? A bouncy bundle of fur with a cute nose and twitching ears? Not 20,000 years ago. Just look at this heavyweight bruiser traveling across the plains, with chunky forearms and a face like thunder. It's too big to hop, so it walks on two legs. One piece of advice: don't try to pet it.

The giant short-faced kangaroo lived alongside humans for as long as 30,000 years. Indigenous Australians still tell tales of a huge, long-armed beast that attacked their ancestors. It would have towered over them, particularly when it was stretching to eat from tree branches—on its toes, it was about 10 feet (3 meters) tall!

We're not sure exactly why the giant short-faced kangaroo became extinct. Some scientists think it was because they were hunted by humans. Other scientists think it was because the climate became drier, which made it much harder for the kangaroos to find water. One other possible reason is that humans set fire to the forests where the animals fed, ruining their food supply.

It's not hard to see how giant short-faced kangaroos got their name. They had snubby snouts and forward-facing eyes—and they weighed about five times as much as a modern kangaroo! This didn't stop them from traveling, though. Australia is an enormous country, and their bones have been discovered far and wide.

SCIENTIFIC NAME
Procoptodon goliah

WEIGHT
Around 450 pounds (200 kg)

WHEN DID IT BECOME EXTINCT?
Around 15,000 years ago

WHERE DID IT LIVE?
Australia

Today's kangaroos graze on grass and plants from the ground, but these prehistoric 'roos were very different. They browsed on trees and bushes, using their clawed hands to grab fistfuls of chewy leaves. Unlike modern kangaroos, they had just one toe on each foot. But as you can see from the picture, even in the Stone Age they carried their babies in a pouch on their stomach!

EUROPEAN HIPPO

HERE COMES TROUBLE. Today, the river Thames flows through the heart of London, passing royal palaces, busy traffic, and noisy markets. Rewind about 150,000 years, however, and the scene was very different. The riverbanks were wild and marshy, and wallowing in the reeds was an extra-large mammal with an extra-large appetite—the European hippo.

These days, hippos live only in the warm climate of Africa, but back in the Stone Age, they were also found across many parts of Europe. The continent's prehistoric wildlife was very different from the animals that live there today—and this big-bellied mud-lover is the number-one example.

It's thought that hippos arrived in Europe from Africa and lived in the rivers there for more than a million years. This tells us that they found enough grass and fruit to feed on and that they were able to exist alongside other big beasts such as mammoths and woolly rhinos.

Europe was warmer back then—but when the climate became colder, many creatures found it hard to survive. By 125,000 years ago, there were no European hippos left.

Humans would have feared the hippo, but we know they also saw it as prey. Hippos wouldn't have been easy to hunt—each one weighed about as much as a killer whale!

SCIENTIFIC NAME
Hippopotamus antiquus

WEIGHT
Around 7,000 pounds (3,200 kg)

WHEN DID IT BECOME EXTINCT?
Around 125,000 years ago

WHERE DID IT LIVE?
Across Europe

SIBERIAN UNICORN

LOOK AT THIS JUGGERNAUT WITH ITS HORN HELD HIGH.

The barrel-shaped body you see here belongs to a prehistoric rhino known as a Siberian unicorn. Unicorns in fairy tales are normally dainty and elegant, but this spectacular real-life beast was a gigantic mass of fur and muscle. It was far bigger and heavier than today's rhinos.

The Siberian unicorn was well adapted to Stone Age life. Its shaggy coat kept it warm on the cold and windy grasslands. Experts think it used its huge horn to defend itself and to sweep snow off the grass and plants in winter. The horn was made of keratin—just like your fingernails!

People used to think that the last Siberian unicorn died between 100,000 and 200,000 years ago. Then scientists found more fossils and discovered that this species was still alive just 39,000 years ago! It's exciting that after all this time, we can still learn new things about prehistoric creatures.

The Siberian unicorn had a large hump on its shoulders, but the extra weight didn't slow it down. Scientists say the animal was probably a fast runner, so if humans got too close, it likely would have been able to chase them away. Can you picture it stamping through the snow, snorting as it goes?

A creature this big would have had a jumbo appetite. Siberian unicorns used their strong teeth to munch on tough, dry grass. But when the Earth warmed up at the end of the last ice age, there wasn't as much grass to eat. This is possibly why it became extinct. We don't have any evidence they were hunted by humans. Maybe our ancestors were scared off by their horns!

SCIENTIFIC NAME
Elasmotherium sibiricum

WEIGHT
Around 9,000 pounds (4,000 kg)

WHEN DID IT BECOME EXTINCT?
Around 39,000 years ago

WHERE DID IT LIVE?
Eastern Europe and western Asia

27

HAAST'S EAGLE

KEEP YOUR EYES ON THE SKIES. This feathery heavyweight was the largest eagle of all time, with a deadly hooked beak and claws as big as a tiger's. The biggest eagle alive today weighs around 18 pounds (8 kilograms)—the Haast's eagle was almost twice as heavy! End to end, its mighty wings stretched farther across than the length of your bed.

It would have taken a very brave person to hunt a Haast's eagle. In fact, some scientists think these eagles might have tried to catch humans! A Haast's eagle would have been powerful enough to snatch a child from the ground.

These giant birds flew above the mountains and lakes of New Zealand for around a million years, striking from above to catch their prey. Being attacked by a Haast's eagle would have been like being hit by a concrete block dropped from a rooftop! But there was a reason why they had to be so strong: they fed on flightless birds called moas, some of which were almost twice the size of ostriches.

Humans arrived in New Zealand around 700 years ago, sailing there from islands in the Pacific Ocean. Can you imagine what they thought when they first saw a Haast's eagle flapping over their heads? But these people started eating the same creatures that the eagles did: moas. When there were no moas left, the eagles were left without the food they needed.

SCIENTIFIC NAME
Hieraaetus moorei

WEIGHT
Up to 33 pounds (15 kg)

WHEN DID IT BECOME EXTINCT?
Around 600 years ago

WHERE DID IT LIVE?
New Zealand

The Māori were the first people to live in New Zealand, and many still live there. Their ancestors left proof that they saw Haast's eagles. In a rock shelter known as Te Ana Pouakai, or the Cave of the Eagle, is a picture of a giant eagle, painted hundreds of years ago.

GLYPTODON

RUMBLING THROUGH THE ANCIENT WOODS COMES A BOULDER ON LEGS. This titanic tank is *Glyptodon*, which humans would have quickly learned was no ordinary leaf-muncher. The creature's head, tail, and body were covered in rock-hard plates and a massive shell, giving it an almost impenetrable suit of armor. Scientists think it could have used its heavy spiked tail as a club.

Glyptodon was slow-moving, but it needed lots of food. Plants, berries, and the dead bodies of other creatures would all have been on the menu! Fully grown, they weighed as much as a car, but even so, early humans would have seen them as prey. One theory is that Stone Age people used empty *Glyptodon* shells to shelter from stormy weather—like a prehistoric umbrella!

In 2017, a professor and her students at Wesleyan University in Connecticut were shocked when they found a wooden crate with a giant object shaped like a pine cone inside. It was a fossil cast of a *Glyptodon* tail! After finding the shell in another crate, they cleaned and displayed the casts—more than sixty years after the parts had been stored and forgotten.

Toward the back of its mouth, *Glyptodon*'s teeth were big and tough, with thick ridges along each side: perfect for grinding foliage and other chewy food. The word *Glyptodon* means "carved tooth."

SCIENTIFIC NAME
Glyptodon

WEIGHT
Up to 4,400 pounds (2,000 kg)

WHEN DID IT BECOME EXTINCT?
Around 10,000 years ago

WHERE DID IT LIVE?
North and South America

It's likely that *Glyptodon* was hunted to extinction by humans, who wanted its meat and shell. Its turtle-like legs didn't allow it to run very fast, and its soft underbelly was vulnerable to sharp weapons.

GIANT LEMUR

EVERYONE LOVES LEMURS. They're cute, they're curious, and they spring from tree to tree like mini-gymnasts. But they weren't always small and stripy-tailed. When humans first arrived on Madagascar, they would have seen this gorilla-size hulk shuffling through the forests on all fours: the largest lemur of all time. With a skull bigger than a basketball and limbs as thick as logs, the giant lemur would have needed plenty of food to stay strong. It was an herbivore, so the plant-rich woodlands of Madagascar were the perfect place for it. Not many of its bones have been found, which could mean that this magnificent creature was a rare one.

The giant lemur became extinct not long after humans arrived on the island. The same happened to all the other megafauna (large animals) that once lived in Madagascar, including the elephant bird (pages 12–13). Because of this, we can be almost certain that giant lemurs disappeared after humans began hunting them and clearing the woodland.

By studying the teeth of the giant lemur, scientists have found that it liked eating leaves from high tree branches rather than stooping down to feed on bushes and grasses.

Madagascar is the only place in the world where lemurs are found in the wild, and more than one hundred different species live on the island today. Thousands of years ago there would have been even more, including several kinds of big sloth lemurs that probably hung upside down from branches!

SCIENTIFIC NAME
Archaeoindris fontoynontii

WEIGHT
Around 440 pounds (200 kg)

WHEN DID IT BECOME EXTINCT?
Around 2,400 years ago

WHERE DID IT LIVE?
Madagascar

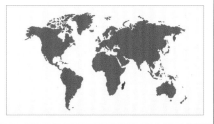

STELLER'S SEA COW

THERE'S A GIANT IN THE WATER. If you were sailing the icy seas between Russia and Alaska 10,000 years ago, you might have spotted one of these supersize swimmers. In fact, they were still living there until 1768! Steller's sea cows were bigger than some of today's whales, with balloon-shaped bodies and short flippers. A sea cow weighed more than two cars put together! But they were very gentle beasts. They spent their time bobbing in the waves and grazing the seabed for seaweed. They didn't even have any teeth—instead, they chewed their food using rough bony pads inside their mouth. Their thick coat of blubber kept them warm.

Steller's sea cows were named after a German explorer, Georg Steller, who was the first person to write a description of the animals. Despite their name, these giant creatures weren't related to the cows we see on land.

One of the closest living relatives of the Steller's sea cow is a peaceful sea mammal called the dugong. Dugongs are much smaller and live in the warm waters of the Indian Ocean, but they have the same whiskery faces and dolphin-like tails.

Because these slow-moving mammals swam in herds, they were easy targets for sailors. Apparently a single sea cow could feed a crew of thirty-three men for a month! Hunting is the likely cause of their final extinction, which occurred less than thirty years after Steller wrote about them.

SCIENTIFIC NAME
Hydrodamalis gigas

WEIGHT
Up to 13,000 pounds (5,900 kg)

WHEN DID IT BECOME EXTINCT?
More than 250 years ago

WHERE DID IT LIVE?
The Bering Sea, between Russia and North America

GIANT WOMBAT

IMAGINE A CUDDLY TOY AS BIG AS YOUR BEDROOM.

Move aside for the giant wombat, a huge, hairy herbivore that wandered the Stone Age wilderness of Australia. These creatures existed alongside humans for thousands of years, and many scientists think they lived and moved in herds. Can you imagine a woodland full of giant wombats, all gobbling greenery and snorting clouds of hot breath? What a sight that would have been!

Like today's much smaller wombats, giant wombats had bulky bodies, moved on four legs, and had big, strong teeth for chewing plants. They were a type of mammal called a marsupial, which means the mothers carried their babies in a pouch on their belly. The giant wombat was the largest marsupial ever!

Hundreds of giant wombat skeletons have been found on the same dry lake bed in South Australia. One theory is that the animals weighed so much that they got stuck in the soft mud when they went looking for water thousands of years ago.

Early humans didn't have the weapons to kill adult giant wombats, so they might have targeted youngsters instead, with spears. But this wasn't the only reason these wombats became extinct. The hot weather made water hard to find, and when humans burned trees and plants, the creatures had less food. Tooth marks on wombat skeletons show they might also have been hunted by big cats.

SCIENTIFIC NAME
Diprotodon

WEIGHT
More than 6,000 pounds (2,700 kg)

WHEN DID IT BECOME EXTINCT?
Around 25,000 years ago

WHERE DID IT LIVE?
Australia

GIANT GROUND SLOTH

SHHH. LISTEN! CAN YOU HEAR THE BRANCHES BEING TORN AND SHAKEN?

This huge, hungry leaf-eater is a giant ground sloth. Imagine a creature as heavy as a truck, with claws like swords and a tail like a dinosaur's. The sloths we know today are slow, sleepy, and rather small, but their ancestors were big enough to rip trees from the soil!

Giant ground sloths roamed across South America for hundreds of thousands of years. If they wanted to reach very high branches, they could sit back on their tails and balance on their hind legs. Some experts even think they could move around on two feet—would you feel nervous if you heard one walking through the trees?

Experts have found ancient sloth bones with tool marks on them, which shows us that the animals were hunted by humans. Sloth skins could be made into clothes by drying the hides, then cutting them into shape. The clothes would have been smelly, but warm! Humans are one of the most likely reasons the sloths became extinct.

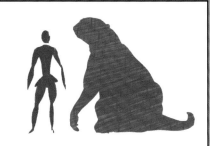

SCIENTIFIC NAME
Megatherium americanum

WEIGHT
Up to 8,800 pounds (4,000 kg)

WHEN DID IT BECOME EXTINCT?
Around 10,500 years ago

WHERE DID IT LIVE?
South America

Hunting a giant ground sloth would have been risky. A swipe of its claws could cause a deadly injury—and there were no hospitals in the Stone Age! But it wasn't just humans that stalked them. If a sloth was too old to defend itself, other beasts would move in for the kill. For predators like saber-toothed cats, a sloth this large would provide a meal that lasted for weeks.

Giant ground sloths had razor-sharp claws, which were perfect for grabbing at branches and leaves. But the claws were so long that the sloths had to curl them inward and walk on the sides of their feet! The animals also had big, square teeth for chewing plants and grasses.

DIRE WOLF

THIS IS NOT THE BIGGEST BEAST IN THE BOOK. It's not the strongest, the tallest, or the heaviest . . . but it might just be the fiercest. Meet the dire wolf, the prowling predator of the American plains, a killer with bone-crunching jaws and savage claws. It had speed, power, and stamina, but what made it really dangerous were its friends. Dire wolves, you see, hunted in packs.

Dire wolves were creatures to fear. They had larger muscles than today's wolves, and their super-sharp teeth would have been vicious weapons. And they also had strength in numbers. It's likely that packs of dire wolves chased down bison, and maybe even young mammoths and mastodons.

The sticky La Brea Tar Pits in California are famous for their animal remains. Many creatures became trapped here in the Stone Age, and the pits show us just how common dire wolves were in the area. Archaeologists have found bears, lions, sloths, and saber-toothed cats—and more than 3,500 dire wolves!

Native American peoples lived alongside dire wolves for thousands of years. The humans would have seen the wolves as a threat. Can you imagine how it would have felt to come face-to-face with a hungry pack in the moonlight, their lips snarling and drooling?

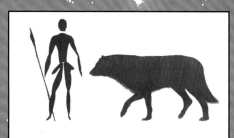

SCIENTIFIC NAME
Aenocyon dirus

WEIGHT
Up to 175 pounds (80 kg)

WHEN DID IT BECOME EXTINCT?
Around 13,000 years ago

WHERE DID IT LIVE?
North and South America

Experts think that the reason for the dire wolves' extinction was . . . extinction! When the slower, larger animals that they hunted became extinct—because of human behavior, climate change, or habitat loss—the wolves found it much harder to survive.

IRISH ELK

THERE ARE TWO THINGS YOU NEED TO KNOW ABOUT THE IRISH ELK. One, its name is a rather strange one, because it didn't live only in Ireland and it wasn't actually an elk. And two, it was the largest deer the world has ever seen, carrying a pair of super-chunky, super-spiky, super-heavy antlers. The creature was found everywhere from the British Isles to the wilds of Siberia.

Only the males balanced these colossal antlers on their heads, and like today's deer, they would have shed them every year and grown a brand-new pair. Scientists say the antlers were used to attract females and to fight off rival males. Can you imagine the rattle and crash of two Irish elk smashing into each other at full speed?

Because Irish elk lived in so many different places, they were seen by many hunter-gatherers across Europe and Asia. The animals would have been prized for their meat and their skin, while their hefty bones and antlers could have been made into valuable tools.

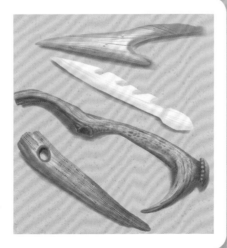

For thousands of years, humans forgot all about these enormous deer. Then, about 500 years ago, villagers in Ireland started finding their fossilized bones. Before long, these giant animals had become famous. King Charles II of England had a pair of ancient antlers mounted on the wall of his palace!

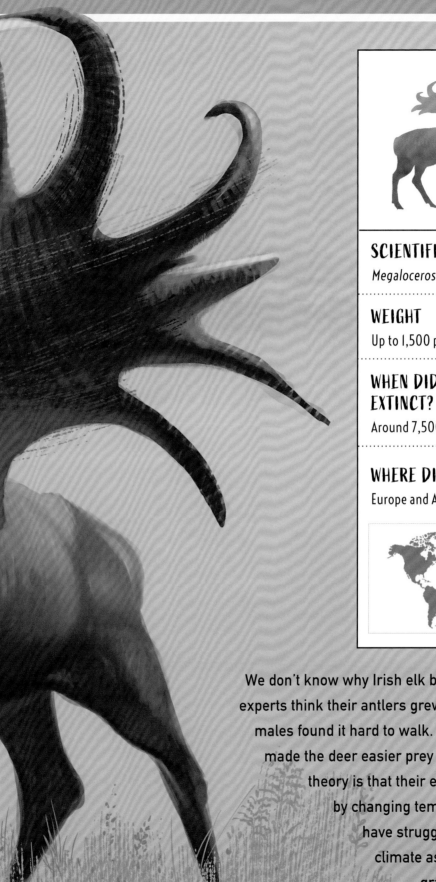

SCIENTIFIC NAME
Megaloceros giganteus

WEIGHT
Up to 1,500 pounds (700 kg)

WHEN DID IT BECOME EXTINCT?
Around 7,500 years ago

WHERE DID IT LIVE?
Europe and Asia

We don't know why Irish elk became extinct. Some experts think their antlers grew so massive that the males found it hard to walk. This would also have made the deer easier prey for humans. Another theory is that their extinction was caused by changing temperatures. They may have struggled to adapt to a new climate as the grasslands they grazed on disappeared.

CAVE LION

MAKE WAY FOR THE KING. This swaggering prehistoric predator might not have had a huge mane, but it had plenty of muscle. The cave lion was one of the largest big cats of all time. It was bulkier and longer than today's African lions, measuring more than 6 feet (2 meters) from its nose to the base of its tail.

Although its bones have been found deep in caves, which is how it got its name, scientists don't think that this cat actually lived underground. It's more likely that it crept inside to hunt the cubs of cave bears. If a mother bear appeared, it would have been a fight to the death.

In 2015, two frozen cave lion cubs were found buried under ice in Russia. The cold temperatures had preserved them for more than 50,000 years! By examining their fur, scientists were able to tell that cave lions were probably a smoky gray color.

SCIENTIFIC NAME
Panthera spelaea

WEIGHT
Up to 700 pounds (300 kg)

WHEN DID IT BECOME EXTINCT?
Around 12,000 years ago

WHERE DID IT LIVE?
Europe and Asia

We know some of these animals lived in France, because beautiful prehistoric cave paintings of the lions have been discovered there. Humans would have been afraid of the fast, fearless lions, but some experts say people killed the animals for their pelts, or skins.

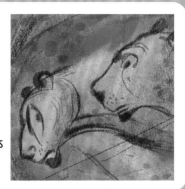

Humans and cave lions almost certainly hunted a lot of the same animals. We don't know why the cave lion became extinct, but maybe it was because humans saw them as competition.

CONCLUSION

WHY DID THESE GIANTS DISAPPEAR?

Many animals that lived during the Stone Age are still with us today, from squirrels and rabbits to bison and crocodiles—but many more are extinct, including all the creatures in this book. As we've seen, there are different reasons why so many of these prehistoric big beasts died out. The Stone Age climate went through many changes, which some large animals and plants were unable to survive, and this had a big impact on food chains and landscapes around the world.

Sadly, the other main reason was humans. Large animals like the ones in this book would have been obvious targets for hunters, either because they were very valuable prey or because they were seen as a threat. Our ancestors understood that they needed to hunt wildlife and clear forests to stay alive, but at the same time they caused many species to disappear forever.

HOW DO WE KNOW SO MUCH ABOUT THESE ANIMALS?

Scientists and archaeologists have very clever ways of knowing how Stone Age animals lived, and what happened to them. For example, if they find a bone with blade marks on it, they can conclude that the animal was butchered and eaten. Or if they find teeth that are square and flat, they can conclude that the animal was a plant-eater.

There are still many things we don't know about prehistoric wildlife, but exciting discoveries are being made every year. When bones and fossils are left in the ground, they often stay well preserved. When they're dug up, some of them hold brand-new information from thousands or even millions of years ago—so who knows what we'll discover next about the amazing animals that once shared our world!

GLOSSARY

ARCHAEOLOGIST

Someone who studies past human life by searching for old objects that people have left behind.

CARNIVORE

An animal that eats only meat.

CLIMATE

Describes weather characteristics over a long period of time. If the climate changes, it means normal temperatures and rainfall start to follow new patterns.

EXTINCT

No longer in existence. If a species of animal or plant dies out completely, it becomes extinct.

FOSSILS

The remains or imprints of animals and plants that lived long ago. Most fossils are found underground.

HABITAT

The place where an animal lives, like a forest, a desert, or grassland. Different habitats are home to different animals.

HERBIVORE

An animal that eats only plants.

HUNTER-GATHERER

Someone who hunts and gathers! A hunter-gatherer survives by finding wild plants and animals to eat.

INDIGENOUS

Used to describe the original or earliest known inhabitants of a particular place.

MEGAFAUNA

Giant animals. *Mega* means very large, and *fauna* means the animals of a particular place.

PREDATOR

An animal that kills and eats another animal.

PREHISTORIC

Belonging to a time before written history. All dinosaurs and Stone Age animals are prehistoric creatures.

PREY

An animal that is killed and eaten by a predator.

SCIENTIFIC NAME

The "official" name that biologists give to a species of animal or plant, usually using Latin or Greek words. For example, the scientific name for a lion is *Panthera leo*.

STONE AGE

The long prehistoric period when stone tools started to be made and used. It was followed by the Bronze Age and the Iron Age.